SHARKS

3-D

Throughout this book, you will find 3-D pictures to explore. Look for the 3-D glasses symbol to find them! To view the pictures, remove the 3-D glasses from the book cover and then hold the red lens over your left eye and the blue lens over your right eye. Watch as the picture comes to life!

i explore

SHARKS

make
believe
ideas

Picture credits: **Nature Picture Library:** 01116286 – Doug Perrine: front cover, p9; 01176197 – Florian Graner: p23;
01226920 – Alex Hyde: p21; 01230136 – Dan Burton: p13. **SeaPics:** 002572 © Mark Strickland / SeaPics.com: pp16–17;
002842 © Marty Snyderman / SeaPics.com: pp24–25; 009577 © Peter Kragh / SeaPics.com: pp14–15;
009717 Copyright © Mark Conlin / SeaPics.com: p17; 011181 © Howard Hall / SeaPics.com: p19;
027530 © C & M Fallows / SeaPics.com: p8, p30; 089497 © Andy Murch / SeaPics.com: pp22–23.

Written by Hayley Down.
With thanks to John Richardson.

Reading together

This book is an ideal first reader for your child, combining simple words and sentences with stunning color photography. Here are some of the many ways you can help your child take those first steps in reading. Encourage your child to:

- Look at and explore the detail in the pictures.
- Sound out the letters in each word.
- Read and repeat each short sentence.

Look at the pictures

Make the most of each page by talking about the pictures and finding key words. Here are some questions you can use to discuss each page as you go along:

- Which photo do you like most? Why?
- What is different about this shark?
- What do you think it would feel like to touch?

Sound out the words

Encourage your child to sound out the letters in any words he or she does not know. Look at the common "key" words listed at the back of the book and see which of them your child can find on each page.

Check for understanding

It is one thing to understand the meaning of individual words, but you need to make sure that your child understands the facts in the text.

- Play "find the obvious mistake." Read the text as your child looks at the words with you, but make an obvious mistake to see if he or she catches it. Ask your child to correct you and provide the right word.
- After reading the facts, close the book and think up questions to ask your child.
- Ask your child whether a fact is true or false.
- Provide your child with three answers to a question and ask him or her to pick the correct one.

Dictionary and key words

At the end of the book, there is a dictionary page to help your child increase his or her vocabulary. There is also a key words page to reinforce your child's knowledge of the most common words.

SHARKS

There are about 450 types of sharks, including the great white shark, the whale shark, and the zebra shark!

back

belly

fin

Zebra shark

i fact

Most sharks have dark skin on their back and pale skin on their belly.

GREAT WHITE SHARK

With its sharp teeth and strong body, the great white shark is an excellent hunter.

i fact

Sharks don't chew their food – they swallow it whole or in large chunks!

snout

tooth

A shark has rows of teeth. When one tooth falls out, another tooth moves to the front to take its place.

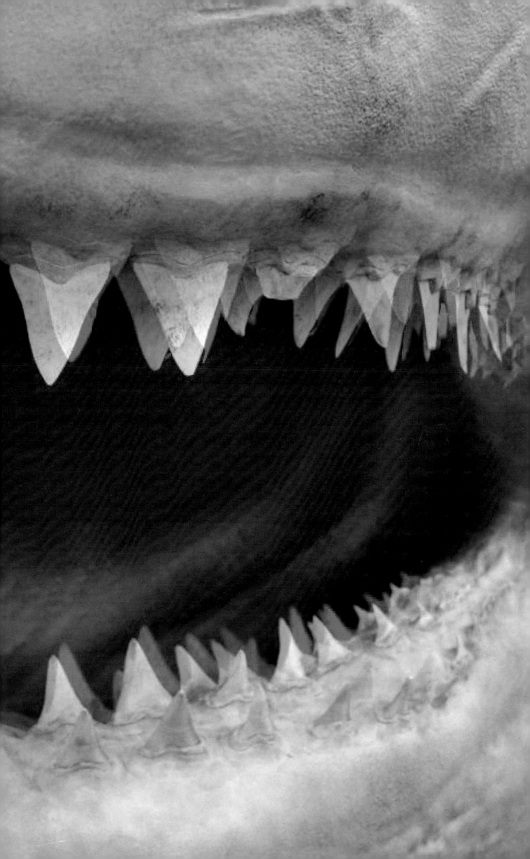

WHALE SHARK

The whale shark is the biggest fish in the world. It eats tiny plants and animals, so it is not a threat to humans.

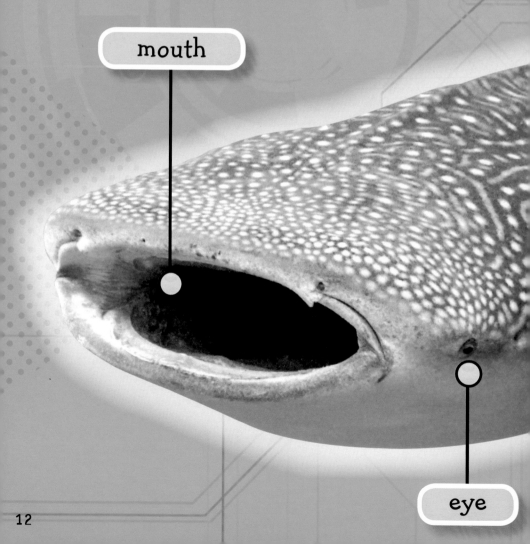

mouth

eye

Whale sharks and basking sharks only swim at about the speed that a person walks.

Basking shark feeding

HAMMERHEAD SHARK

The hammerhead shark takes its name from its hammer-shaped head!

i A hammer-shaped head makes it easier for the shark to move through the water and change direction while swimming.

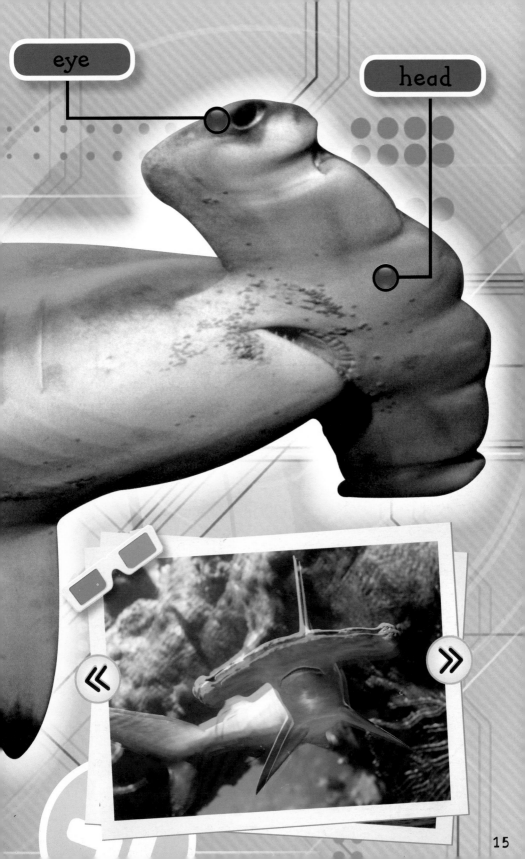

eye

head

15

Most sharks know how to
hunt without being taught.
When a silvertip shark is born,
it has to look after itself
right away.

mother shark

baby shark

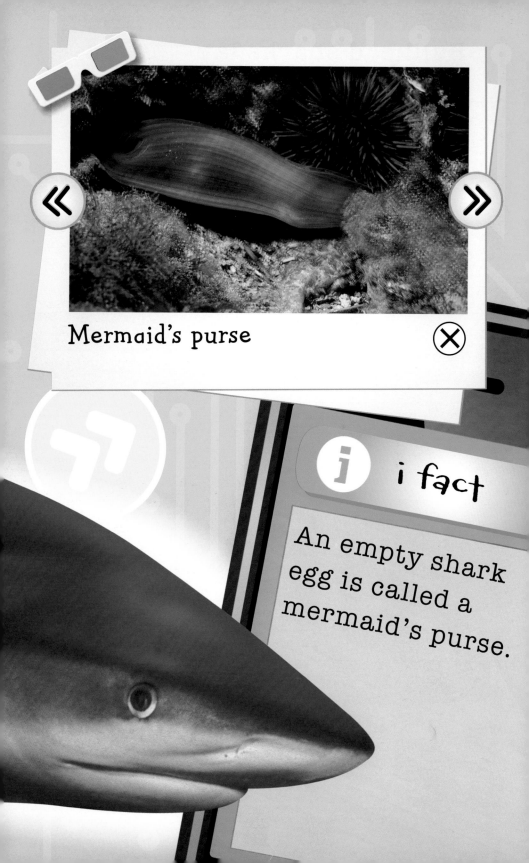

Mermaid's purse

i fact

An empty shark egg is called a mermaid's purse.

Bullhead sharks lay a spiral-shaped egg. They push the egg between rocks to keep it safe.

Bullhead shark hatching

BLACKTIP REEF SHARK

The blacktip reef shark has black patches at the ends of its fins. It lives in shallow water on coral reefs.

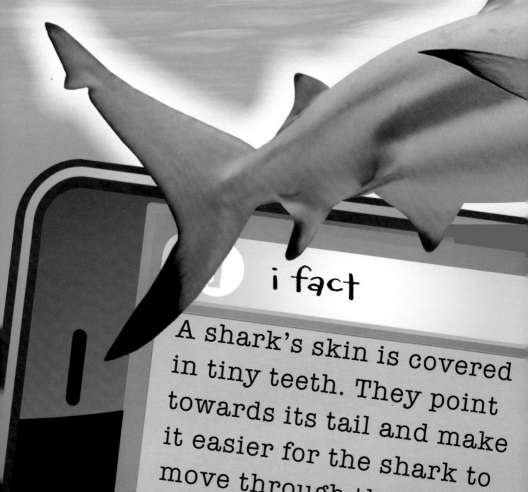

i fact

A shark's skin is covered in tiny teeth. They point towards its tail and make it easier for the shark to move through the water.

Shark's skin

nostril

fin

UNUSUAL SHARKS

Some sharks do not look like sharks at all. The tasselled wobbegong shark has a beard made of whiskers that look like seaweed.

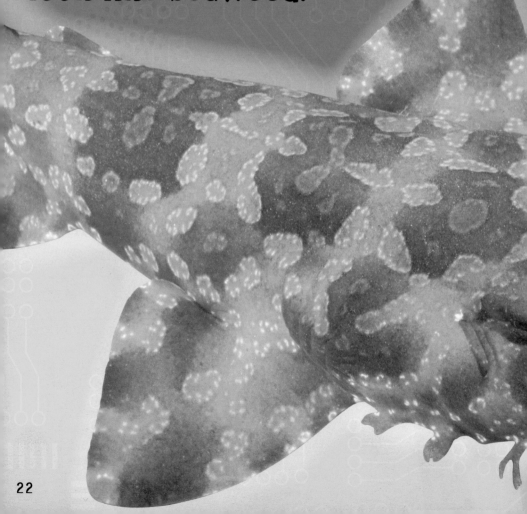

The dwarf lantern shark only grows to 8 in (21 cm) long. That's about the size of an adult's hand!

Dwarf lantern shark

mouth

whiskers

A saw shark has a long snout with teeth along the edges. It uses its snout to kill other fish.

ENDANGERED SHARKS

Many sharks are endangered, like the scalloped hammerhead shark. This means they are at risk of dying out completely.

Great white shark

scalloped hammerhead shark

eye

mouth

i i fact

Even the great white shark is at risk because its numbers are falling.

Sharks try their food before they eat it. If the food is too bony for them, they let it go.

Every year, more people die from beestings than from shark attacks.

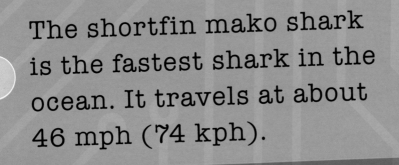

The shortfin mako shark is the fastest shark in the ocean. It travels at about 46 mph (74 kph).

Sharks were around before the dinosaurs!

DICTIONARY

fins

Fins are flat, thin body parts.
Fish, including sharks, have fins.

hunter

A hunter is an animal that chases
and kills other animals for food.

nostril

A nostril is a hole in the nose
of an animal or person.
We smell through our nostrils.

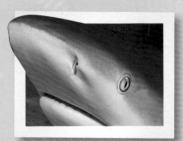

snout

A snout sticks out from an
animal's head and is both
its nose and its mouth.

threat

When something is a threat,
it is dangerous.

Here are some key words used in context. Help your child to use other words from the border in simple sentences.

When a shark's tooth falls out, another tooth takes its place.

Great white sharks are good **at** hunting.

Most sharks **have** dark skin on their back.

You are more likely to be hurt by a bee than by a shark.

They are sharks.